MW00426845

Fearless

Confidence Journal for the Female Hustler

The Fearless Journal is for the goal digger, the go getter, the hustler, the woman who is a visionary.

Being fearless as a woman is major for your confidence. Taking risks where you don't see a clear end result is brave. I want you to be more fearless this year. There is so much you will accomplish in the upcoming months.

JUST FOCUS

The purpose of this journal is to build the habit of journaling as well as increase your confidence. You are what you do consistently. I started journaling in 2016, and since then I've accomplished all of the fearless goals I had for myself. I want the same for you. I want you to reach your goals as bad as you want to breathe.

#yougotthis

Your ideas are game changing. Your goals are attainable. Your hustle is unmatched. These attributes matched with fearlessness will take you far.

You are a fearless woman.

Fearless Journal

Confidence Journal for the Female Hustler

be fearless in the pursuit of what sets your soul on fire

CREATED BY: INDIA K. LINDSEY

Building the Habit

HABIT TRACKER: We want to build healthy habits and consistency. The habit tracker will appear every seven pages. It is intended to do one every seven days. Do you want to exercise more, write more, journal more or drink more water? Use this section to keep track of your habits.

DATE/LOCATION: In this section, write out the date, time and location you are journaling. When you look back at your entries, knowing where you were when you wrote them will motivate you to continue to document.

REFLECTION: Reflect on the beginning, middle or end of your day. I added journal prompts on every other day to help you get started and to get your mind flowing to write.

FEARLESS GOAL: Always have a fearless goal you are working towards, it can be as simple as journaling more everyday.

Goals

- ☐ _____
- ☐ _____
- ☐ _____
- ☐ _____
- ☐ _____
- ☐ _____

DATES TO REMEMBER

IMPORTANT NOTES

my weekly habits

HABIT TRACKER

M T W T F S

☐ ☐ ☐ ☐ ☐ ☐

☐ ☐ ☐ ☐ ☐ ☐

☐ ☐ ☐ ☐ ☐ ☐

☐ ☐ ☐ ☐ ☐ ☐

☐ ☐ ☐ ☐ ☐ ☐

☐ ☐ ☐ ☐ ☐ ☐

☐ ☐ ☐ ☐ ☐ ☐

_____

_____

_____

_____

_____

_____

REMINDERS

NOTES

May 16, 2020 - home
IN BED

If you woke up and all of your dreams came true, what changed?

Date/Locatio

Reflection

If I woke up and all of
my dreams came true, I
would wake up stress free.
I would feel secure about my
future with little worries about
unexpected obstacles. right now.

I am in a season of job hunting,
of setting myself up for the future
and wow thats alot. It worries
me a little because I really
just never know what to expect....

Fearless Goal:

Believe IN myself.

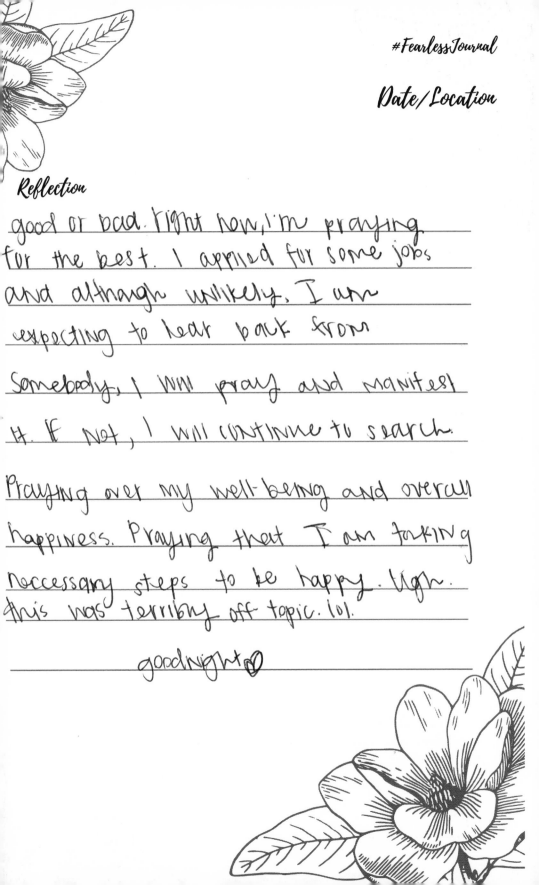

Reflection

good or bad. right now, I'm praying
for the best. I applied for some jobs
and although unlikely, I am
expecting to hear back from
somebody. I will pray and manifest
it. If not, I will continue to search.

Praying over my well-being and overall
happiness. Praying that I am taking
neccessary steps to be happy. Ugh.
this was terribly off topic. lol.

goodnight♡

Have you ever disappointed yourself?

Reflection

_____

_____

_____

_____

_____

_____

_____

_____

_____

_____

_____

_____

Fearless Goal:

Reflection

Describe the happiest day of your life

Reflection

_____

_____

_____

_____

_____

_____

_____

_____

_____

_____

_____

Fearless Goal:

Date/Location

Reflection

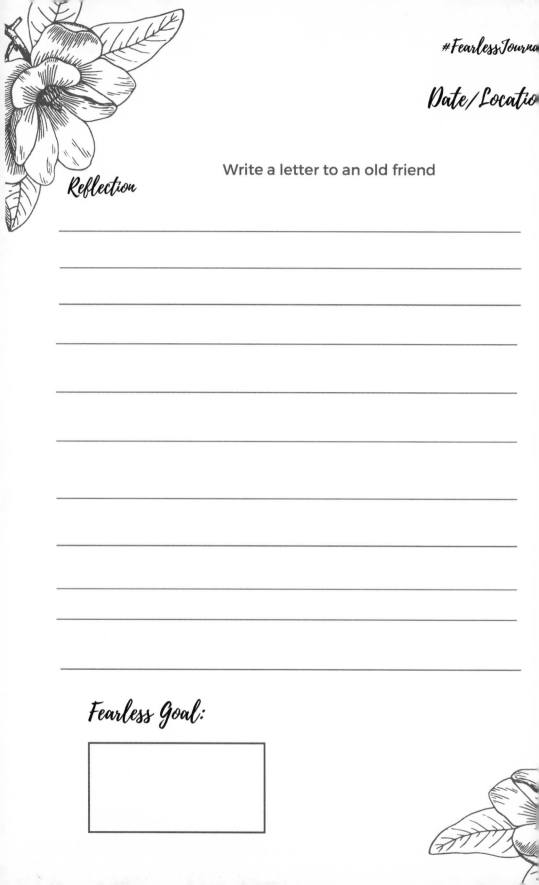

Write a letter to an old friend

Reflection

_____
_____
_____
_____
_____
_____
_____
_____
_____
_____
_____
_____

Fearless Goal:

Women have to work much harder to make it in this world. It really pisses me off that women don't get the same opportunities as men do, or money for that matter. Because let's face it, money gives men the power to run the show. It gives men the power to define our values and to define what's sexy and what's feminine and that's bullshit.

At the end of the day, it's not about equal rights, it's about how we think. We have to reshape our own perception of how we view ourselves. — Beyoncé

my weekly habits

HABIT TRACKER

	M	T	W	T	F	S
_____	☐	☐	☐	☐	☐	☐
_____	☐	☐	☐	☐	☐	☐
_____	☐	☐	☐	☐	☐	☐
_____	☐	☐	☐	☐	☐	☐
_____	☐	☐	☐	☐	☐	☐
_____	☐	☐	☐	☐	☐	☐
	☐	☐	☐	☐	☐	☐

REMINDERS

NOTES

Date/Location

If you wrote a book about your life, how would it go?

Reflection

_____
_____
_____
_____
_____
_____
_____
_____
_____
_____
_____
_____

Fearless Goal:

Date/Locatio

Reflection

_____

_____

_____

_____

_____

_____

_____

_____

_____

_____

_____

_____

Date/Location

Where do you see yourself in five years?

Reflection

_____

_____

_____

_____

_____

_____

_____

_____

_____

_____

_____

_____

Fearless Goal:

Date/Locatio

Reflection

_____

_____

_____

_____

_____

_____

_____

_____

_____

_____

_____

Date/Location

Do you feel stuck?
What are some ways you can change your situation?

Reflection

_____

_____

_____

_____

_____

_____

_____

_____

_____

_____

_____

_____

Fearless Goal:

Reflection

_____

_____

_____

_____

_____

_____

_____

_____

_____

_____

_____

Date/Location

What made you smile today?

Reflection

_____

_____

_____

_____

_____

_____

_____

_____

_____

_____

_____

_____

Fearless Goal:

Affirmation:

My self worth is not based on my achievements or accolades. I give myself grace when I make mistakes. Mistakes are a learning opportunity. I enjoy the process and not focus on outcomes. My best is my best. Done beats perfect.

I am imperfect and still enough.

my weekly habits

HABIT TRACKER

M T W T F S

☐ ☐ ☐ ☐ ☐ ☐

☐ ☐ ☐ ☐ ☐ ☐

☐ ☐ ☐ ☐ ☐ ☐

☐ ☐ ☐ ☐ ☐ ☐

☐ ☐ ☐ ☐ ☐ ☐

☐ ☐ ☐ ☐ ☐ ☐

☐ ☐ ☐ ☐ ☐ ☐

REMINDERS

NOTES

If you received $25,000 today, how would you spend it?

Reflection

_____

_____

_____

_____

_____

_____

_____

_____

_____

_____

_____

_____

Fearless Goal:

Date/Location

Reflection

_____
_____
_____
_____
_____
_____
_____
_____
_____
_____
_____

Describe your perfect partner

Reflection

_____

_____

_____

_____

_____

_____

_____

_____

_____

_____

_____

Fearless Goal:

Date/Location

Reflection

Date/Locatio

Are you happy? Why or why not?

Reflection

_____

_____

_____

_____

_____

_____

_____

_____

_____

_____

_____

Fearless Goal:

Date/Location

Reflection

_____
_____
_____
_____
_____
_____
_____
_____
_____
_____
_____

What does romance mean to you?

Reflection

_____

_____

_____

_____

_____

_____

_____

_____

_____

_____

_____

Fearless Goal:

The present is a gift. Stop looking backwards and stop looking forward. Stop thinking, what if? Stop! Live for today and don't take for granted the gift of the present.

my weekly habits

HABIT TRACKER

	M	T	W	T	F	S
_____	☐	☐	☐	☐	☐	☐
_____	☐	☐	☐	☐	☐	☐
_____	☐	☐	☐	☐	☐	☐
_____	☐	☐	☐	☐	☐	☐
_____	☐	☐	☐	☐	☐	☐
_____	☐	☐	☐	☐	☐	☐
	☐	☐	☐	☐	☐	☐

REMINDERS

NOTES

Date/Location

Reflection

_____

_____

_____

_____

_____

_____

_____

_____

_____

_____

_____

What would you change about your job to make it better?

Reflection

_____

_____

_____

_____

_____

_____

_____

_____

_____

_____

_____

Fearless Goal:

Reflection

Date/Locatio

What is a bad habit you want to break?

Reflection

_____
_____
_____
_____
_____
_____
_____
_____
_____
_____
_____
_____

Fearless Goal:

Date/Location

Reflection

Date/Locatio

Write about the last time you cried

Reflection

_____

_____

_____

_____

_____

_____

_____

_____

_____

_____

_____

_____

_____

Fearless Goal:

Date/Location

Reflection

_____
_____
_____
_____
_____
_____
_____
_____
_____
_____
_____

my weekly habits

HABIT TRACKER

	M	T	W	T	F	S
_____	☐	☐	☐	☐	☐	☐
_____	☐	☐	☐	☐	☐	☐
_____	☐	☐	☐	☐	☐	☐
_____	☐	☐	☐	☐	☐	☐
_____	☐	☐	☐	☐	☐	☐
_____	☐	☐	☐	☐	☐	☐
	☐	☐	☐	☐	☐	☐

REMINDERS

NOTES

Date/Location

What are you looking forward to?

Reflection

_____

_____

_____

_____

_____

_____

_____

_____

_____

_____

_____

_____

Write about your best friend, why are they your best friend?

Reflection

_____

_____

_____

_____

_____

_____

_____

_____

_____

_____

_____

Date/Location

What are you stressed about right now ?

Reflection

_____

_____

_____

_____

_____

_____

_____

_____

_____

_____

_____

_____

Fearless Goal:

Notes

my weekly habits

HABIT TRACKER

	M	T	W	T	F	S
_____	☐	☐	☐	☐	☐	☐
_____	☐	☐	☐	☐	☐	☐
_____	☐	☐	☐	☐	☐	☐
_____	☐	☐	☐	☐	☐	☐
_____	☐	☐	☐	☐	☐	☐
_____	☐	☐	☐	☐	☐	☐
	☐	☐	☐	☐	☐	☐

REMINDERS

NOTES

Date/Locatio

Reflection

_____
_____
_____
_____
_____
_____
_____
_____
_____
_____
_____
_____

Date/Location

What is your love language?

Reflection

_____
_____
_____
_____
_____
_____
_____
_____
_____
_____
_____
_____
_____

Fearless Goal:

Date/Locatio

Reflection

_____

_____

_____

_____

_____

_____

_____

_____

_____

_____

_____

my weekly habits

HABIT TRACKER

M T W T F S

_____

_____

_____

_____

_____

_____

REMINDERS

NOTES

Date/Locatio

What is one habit you want to have in the next 30 days?

Reflection

_____

_____

_____

_____

_____

_____

_____

_____

_____

_____

_____

Fearless Goal:

Date/Location

Reflection

_____

_____

_____

_____

_____

_____

_____

_____

_____

_____

_____

_____

List 6 things you want to do in the next 6 months

Reflection

_____

_____

_____

_____

_____

_____

_____

_____

_____

_____

_____

Fearless Goal:

Date/Location

Reflection

Affirmation:

I live in the present. I enjoy every moment I am living. I have closed the chapters from the past. The past is the past and I will leave it there. I'm perfect, how I am today. When I look in the mirror, I see a GODDESS. I do not compare myself or my situation to other people.

my weekly habits

HABIT TRACKER

M T W T F S

_____

_____

_____

_____

_____

_____

REMINDERS

NOTES

Date/Locatio

Talk about the last compliment that made you smile

Reflection

_____

_____

_____

_____

_____

_____

_____

_____

_____

_____

_____

Fearless Goal:

Date/Location

Reflection

_____
_____
_____
_____
_____
_____
_____
_____
_____
_____
_____
_____

Who are the five best people in your life,
What value do they bring?

Reflection

_____

_____

_____

_____

_____

_____

_____

_____

_____

_____

Fearless Goal:

Date/Location

Reflection

Date/Location

What is something you have today that you didn't have a year ago?

Reflection

_____

_____

_____

_____

_____

_____

_____

_____

_____

_____

_____

_____

Fearless Goal:

Date/Location

Reflection

_____

_____

_____

_____

_____

_____

_____

_____

_____

_____

_____

Date/Location

Do you have someone you miss?

Reflection

_____
_____
_____
_____
_____
_____
_____
_____
_____
_____
_____

Fearless Goal:

Reflection

_____

_____

_____

_____

_____

_____

_____

_____

_____

_____

_____

What do you love and appreciate about yourself?

Reflection

_____

_____

_____

_____

_____

_____

_____

_____

_____

_____

_____

Fearless Goal:

Affirmation:
My wants and needs are always being met and taken care of.

I am not afraid to invest in myself and my business because I know that the investments I make will make me successful. All the money I spend comes back to me multiplied

Date/Locatio

Reflection

_____

_____

_____

_____

_____

_____

_____

_____

_____

_____

_____

Date/Location

What can't you stop thinking about ?

Reflection

_____

_____

_____

_____

_____

_____

_____

_____

_____

_____

_____

_____

Fearless Goal:

Date/Locatio

Reflection

_____
_____
_____
_____
_____
_____
_____
_____
_____
_____
_____

Date/Location

Reflect on a small miracle that changed your life

Reflection

_____

_____

_____

_____

_____

_____

_____

_____

_____

_____

_____

_____

Fearless Goal:

my weekly habits

HABIT TRACKER

	M	T	W	T	F	S
_____	☐	☐	☐	☐	☐	☐
_____	☐	☐	☐	☐	☐	☐
_____	☐	☐	☐	☐	☐	☐
_____	☐	☐	☐	☐	☐	☐
_____	☐	☐	☐	☐	☐	☐
_____	☐	☐	☐	☐	☐	☐
	☐	☐	☐	☐	☐	☐

REMINDERS

NOTES

Date/Locatio

What do you feel guilty about or regret?

Reflection

Fearless Goal:

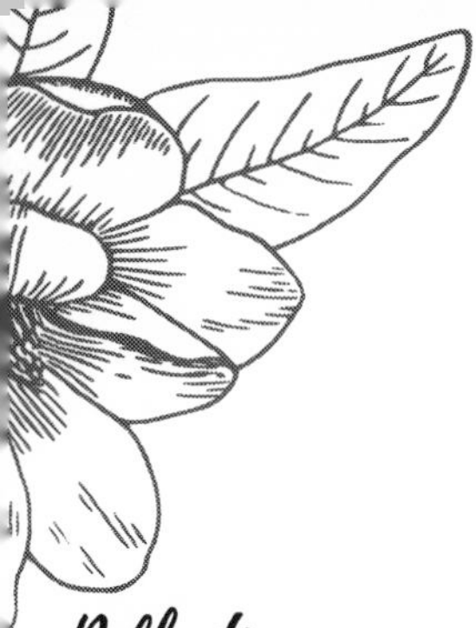

Reflection

_____
_____
_____
_____
_____
_____
_____
_____
_____
_____
_____
_____
_____
_____

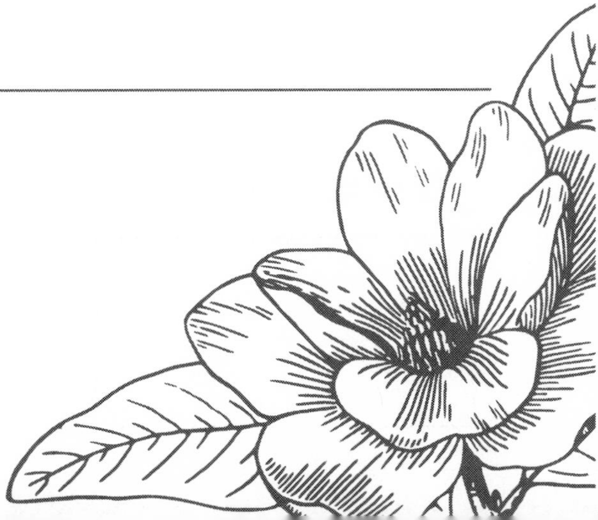

Date/Locatio

What are you scared of?

Reflection

_____

_____

_____

_____

_____

_____

_____

_____

_____

_____

_____

Fearless Goal:

Date/Location

Reflection

Self love is important. Write a love letter to yourself.

Reflection

_____

_____

_____

_____

_____

_____

_____

_____

_____

_____

_____

_____

Fearless Goal:

Date/Location

Reflection

_____

_____

_____

_____

_____

_____

_____

_____

_____

_____

_____

_____

_____

What does success mean to you?

Reflection

_____

_____

_____

_____

_____

_____

_____

_____

_____

_____

_____

Fearless Goal:

Affirmation:

I trust my work and talent enough to charge premium pricing. I'm okay with increasing my prices to match the value I bring. I'm okay with saying no to customers who are not serious about working with me and my brand. Customers are cashing me down with money. I am a successful entrepreneur.

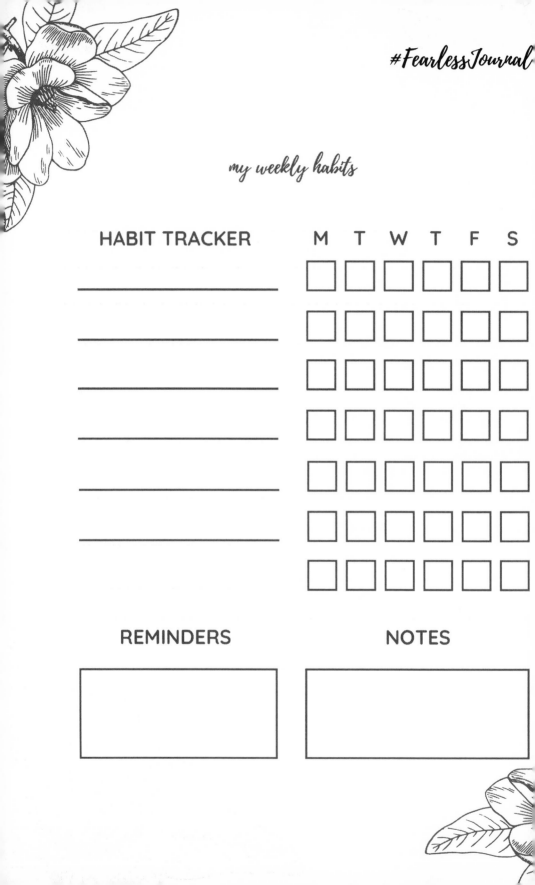

my weekly habits

HABIT TRACKER

	M	T	W	T	F	S
_____	☐	☐	☐	☐	☐	☐
_____	☐	☐	☐	☐	☐	☐
_____	☐	☐	☐	☐	☐	☐
_____	☐	☐	☐	☐	☐	☐
_____	☐	☐	☐	☐	☐	☐
_____	☐	☐	☐	☐	☐	☐
	☐	☐	☐	☐	☐	☐

REMINDERS

NOTES

Reflection

_____
_____
_____
_____
_____
_____
_____
_____
_____
_____
_____
_____
_____

Date/Locatio

Write about the last time you were angry

Reflection

_____

_____

_____

_____

_____

_____

_____

_____

_____

_____

_____

_____

Fearless Goal:

Date/Location

Reflection

_____

_____

_____

_____

_____

_____

_____

_____

_____

_____

_____

If you could learn any language, what would it be?

Reflection

_____

_____

_____

_____

_____

_____

_____

_____

_____

_____

_____

Fearless Goal:

Reflection

_____

_____

_____

_____

_____

_____

_____

_____

_____

_____

_____

_____

Date/Locatio

What are you passionate about?

Reflection

_____
_____
_____
_____
_____
_____
_____
_____
_____
_____
_____
_____

Fearless Goal:

Date/Location

Reflection

_____
_____
_____
_____
_____
_____
_____
_____
_____
_____
_____

Date/Locatio

What are you grateful for?

Reflection

Fearless Goal:

Date/Location

Reflection

Why did your last relationship end?

Reflection

_____

_____

_____

_____

_____

_____

_____

_____

_____

_____

_____

Fearless Goal:

Date/Location

What do you like about your boss?

Reflection

_____

_____

_____

_____

_____

_____

_____

_____

_____

_____

_____

_____

Weekly Habits

HABIT TRACKER

	M	T	W	T	F	S
_____	☐	☐	☐	☐	☐	☐
_____	☐	☐	☐	☐	☐	☐
_____	☐	☐	☐	☐	☐	☐
_____	☐	☐	☐	☐	☐	☐
_____	☐	☐	☐	☐	☐	☐
_____	☐	☐	☐	☐	☐	☐
	☐	☐	☐	☐	☐	☐

REMINDERS

NOTES

Date/Location

What does a fearless woman mean to you?

Reflection

_____

_____

_____

_____

_____

_____

_____

_____

_____

_____

_____

_____

Fearless Goal:

Reflection

_____

_____

_____

_____

_____

_____

_____

_____

_____

_____

Date/Location

Write a letter to yourself 5 years ago

Reflection

_____

_____

_____

_____

_____

_____

_____

_____

_____

_____

_____

_____

_____

Fearless Goal:

Date/Locatio

Reflection

_____
_____
_____
_____
_____
_____
_____
_____
_____
_____
_____

Date/Location

Are you sometimes too hard on yourself?

Reflection

_____
_____
_____
_____
_____
_____
_____
_____
_____
_____
_____

Fearless Goal:

Date/Locatio

Reflection

_____

_____

_____

_____

_____

_____

_____

_____

_____

_____

_____

Notes

India Lindsey, 2019

Made in the USA
Coppell, TX
28 April 2020